Therapy Animals

ABDO
Publishing Company

A Buddy **Book by**
Julie Murray

VISIT US AT
www.abdopublishing.com

Published by ABDO Publishing Company, 8000 West 78th Street, Edina, Minnesota 55439.

Printed in the United States.

Coordinating Series Editor: Rochelle Baltzer
Editor: Sarah Tieck
Contributing Editor: Marcia Zappa
Graphic Design: Maria Hosley
Cover Photograph: *Getty Images:* Stephen Chernin
Interior Photographs/Illustrations: *AP Photo:* Doug Bauman/The Daily Oakland Press (p. 15), Al Behrman (p. 27), Manuel Balce Ceneta (p. 19), Brian Loden/Starkville Daily News (p. 26), Pete Pallagi/Daily News-Sun (p. 9), Tim Roske (pp. 5, 7, 29), Lindsay Wheatley/Iowa State Daily (p. 23); *Getty Images:* Ira Block/National Geographic (p. 17), William Foley/Time Life Pictures (p. 21), Chris Jackson (p. 13); *iStockPhoto:* Dennis Guyitt (p. 13), iofoto (p. 30), Valerie Loiseleux (p. 5), Anna Pustovaya (p. 30); *Photos.com:* Jupiter Images (p. 13); Ron Tyrrell (pp. 5, 25); *Wikipedia.com* (p. 11).

Library of Congress Cataloging-in-Publication Data

Murray, Julie, 1969-
  Therapy animals / Julie Murray.
    p. cm. -- (Going to work. Animal edition)
  ISBN 978-1-60453-565-5
  1. Animals--Therapeutic use--Juvenile literature. I. Title.

  RM931.A65M87 2009
  615.8'5158--dc22

                                                                2008040270

Contents

Animals At Work

Going to work is an important part of life. At work, people use their skills to accomplish tasks and earn money.

Animals can have jobs, too. Many times, they complete tasks that human workers can't. Some even change people's lives.

One job animals have is therapy. Therapy animals lift people's spirits and help them meet **goals**. This is worthwhile work.

Rabbits, dogs, and horses are common therapy animals. But, all kinds of animals can do therapy work!

Helping Out

Therapy animals are pets that help people learn, heal, and **communicate**. They also comfort people and cheer them up. These animals work in hospitals, schools, and other settings.

Therapy animals connect with people in ways human helpers cannot. Many people enjoy working with animals. So, they push themselves to improve.

Therapy animals work in busy settings. There are often unusual sounds and sights. Therapy animals are prepared for these situations.

When therapy animals comfort and cheer people up, they are doing animal-assisted activities (AAA). Usually, **volunteers** and their pets do AAA work.

When animals help people learn and practice skills, it is called animal-assisted therapy (AAT). During AAT, therapists and doctors use animals with **patients**. The animals help people reach **goals**.

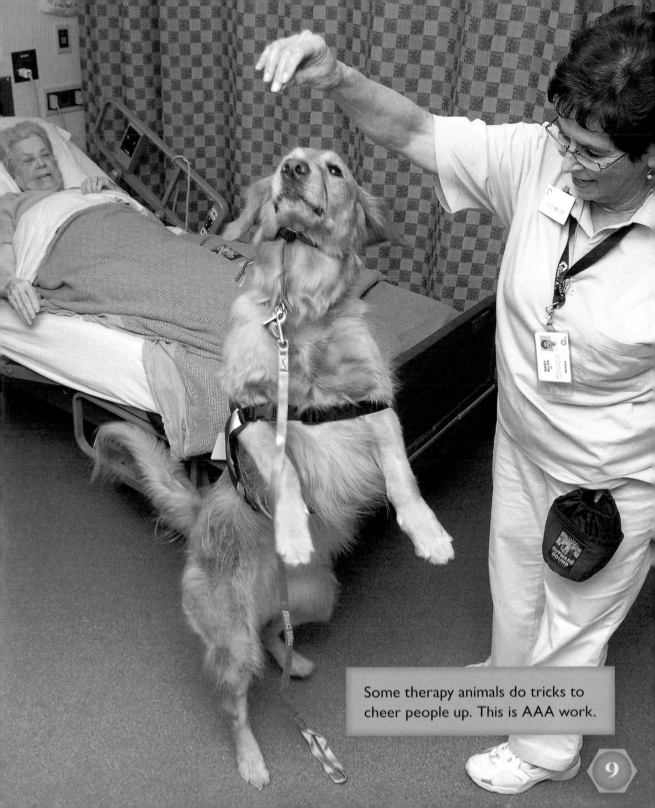

Some therapy animals do tricks to cheer people up. This is AAA work.

HISTORY LESSON

One of the first therapy animals was a Yorkshire terrier named Smoky. She became famous as a **World War II** hero!

At first, Smoky did tricks and cheered soldiers up. Later, she spent time helping wounded soldiers in hospitals.

When Smoky's owner had to stay in the hospital during the war. Smoky was allowed to sleep in his bed. But. she also visited other patients.

Smoky's owner was war photographer William Wynne. He took many pictures of Smoky and even wrote a book about his pet!

Did You Know?

In 1984. Elaine Smith helped write a law in New Jersey. It protected the rights of some helper dogs. Since then. more laws in other states have been passed.

In 1976, U.S. nurse Elaine Smith started Therapy Dogs **International** Inc. In England, Smith had seen hospital **patients** improve when a golden retriever visited. This gave her the idea to start a group.

Smith created opportunities for therapy animals. For years, she and her German shepherd Phila did therapy visits. Smith also helped pass new laws.

One of Smith's goals was to increase the number of therapy dogs. Today, many different dog breeds do therapy work. These include golden retrievers (*top*), German shepherds (*middle*), and dachshunds (*bottom*).

Working Together

Calm, gentle animals are chosen for therapy. They must be comfortable with people. Trainers help animals and their human **partners** learn needed skills.

Training depends on the type of animal. And, the range of therapy jobs require different skills. Trainers teach animals commands and manners.

Each therapy animal has a human partner. Often this partner is the animal's owner. Together, the animal and partner go on therapy visits and attend training sessions.

Helping Paws

Dogs are the most popular therapy animal. They help people in many different ways, including both AAA and AAT work.

Some dogs help out during **disasters** and **emergencies**. They comfort **victims** and emergency workers.

On September 11, 2001, planes crashed into the World Trade Center in New York City, New York. Many people were killed or hurt. Therapy dogs traveled to the scene to cheer up and comfort police officers and firefighters.

17

Dogs are also great listeners! The Reading Education Assistance Dogs (R.E.A.D.) **program** sends dogs and **volunteers** to schools and libraries. The dogs listen to children read stories. Some even turn pages with their paws and noses!

Reading to dogs helps many children relax and feel comfortable. Children who have trouble reading or **communicating** often improve when they read to dogs.

Dogs help some children feel calm and enjoy reading.

Fur And Feathers

Rabbits, cats, birds, and even goats are among the many animals that do AAA work. These animals improve people's moods and ability to connect with others. People are healthier and happier after their visits.

Some animals put on shows or do tricks. Sometimes, people just pet the animals.

Therapy animals travel to many different settings to visit people (*top*). Sometimes, people travel to places, such as farms, to visit therapy animals (*bottom*).

Gentle Friends

Llamas are known for spitting and kicking. But, most are really gentle. Some llamas even work as therapy animals.

Llamas mostly do AAT work. Because llamas are unusual animals, **patients** are often excited to meet them. A person who has trouble moving an arm might work harder to pet a llama.

Large, furry llamas come from South America. They belong to the same animal family as camels.

Hoofed Helpers

Horses are often used for AAA and AAT work. Riding a horse moves a human body in a similar way to walking. So, riding horses helps disabled **patients** gain control and improve balance.

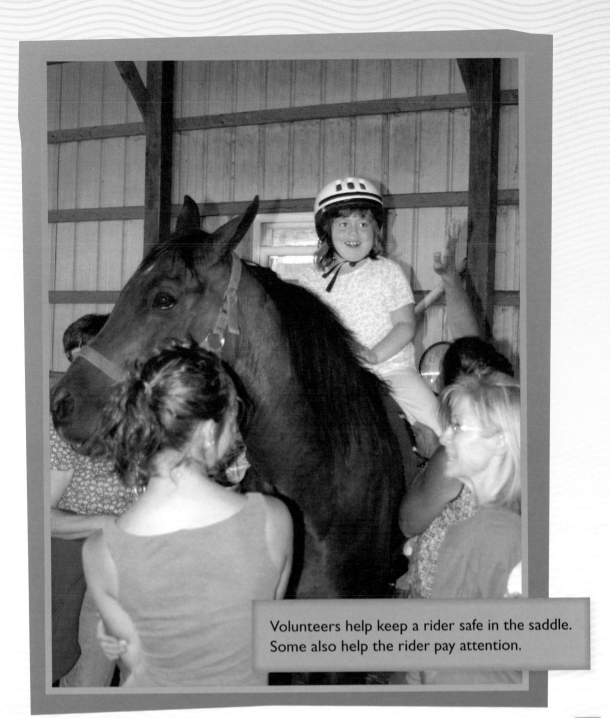

Volunteers help keep a rider safe in the saddle. Some also help the rider pay attention.

Horses move riders up and down and side to side. They also move forward and backward. Riders benefit greatly from this variety of movement.

Horses are used by **mental** health workers, too. **Patients** feel more sure of themselves as they work with horses. They learn useful life skills.

Autistic children have trouble connecting and **communicating** with people. And, children who have attention-deficit/hyperactivity disorder struggle to pay attention. When these children work with horses, they improve.

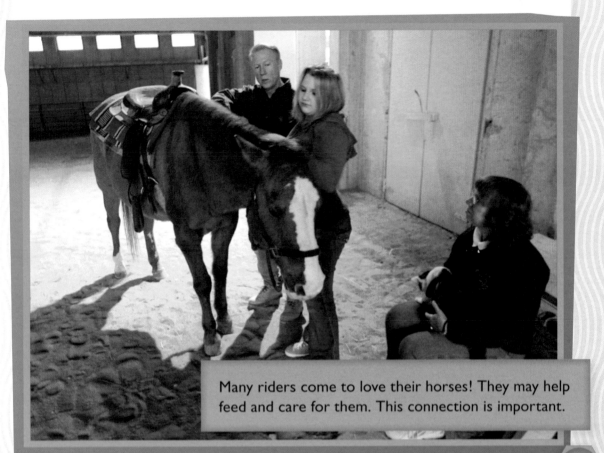

Many riders come to love their horses! They may help feed and care for them. This connection is important.

Gifted Workers

Therapy animals do many important tasks. They work in different settings to help people move, **communicate**, and heal. Therapy animals do special work that improves the lives of many people!

Therapy dogs work with patients of all ages. They are also comfortable with people who may speak loudly or move in unusual ways.

The Animal Times

Splish Splash!

Some people swim with dolphins as a type of therapy. But, many scientists say it is just for fun.

Pet Partners

The Delta Society helps train therapy animals. Its Pet **Partners program** has more than 10,000 animal **volunteer** members across the United States!

Important Words

communicate (kuh-MYOO-nuh-kayt) to share one's knowledge.

disaster (dih-ZAS-tuhr) an event that causes damage and suffering.

emergency (ih-MUHR-juhnt-see) an unexpected event that requires immediate action.

goal (GOHL) something that a person works to accomplish.

international (ihn-tuhr-NASH-nuhl) of or relating to more than one nation.

mental having to do with the mind.

partner a part of a team.

patient (PAY-shuhnt) a person who is under the care of a doctor.

program a plan for doing something.

victim (VIHK-tuhm) a person who has been hurt in an accident or a crime.

volunteer (vah-luhn-TIHR) an unpaid worker.

World War II a war fought in Europe, Asia, and Africa from 1939 to 1945.

Web Sites

To learn more about therapy animals, visit ABDO Publishing Company online. Web sites about therapy animals are featured on our Book Links page. These links are routinely monitored and updated to provide the most current information available.

www.abdopublishing.com

Index